"SHE MET WITH GAFFER WOLF."

HEATH SUPPLEMENTARY READERS

THE TALES OF
MOTHER GOOSE

AS FIRST COLLECTED BY
CHARLES PERRAULT IN 1696

A NEW TRANSLATION BY CHARLES WELSH

INTRODUCTION BY
M. V. O'SHEA

ILLUSTRATED BY D. J. MUNRO
AFTER DRAWINGS BY GUSTAVE DORÉ

D. C. HEATH AND COMPANY
BOSTON   NEW YORK   CHICAGO   ATLANTA
DALLAS   SAN FRANCISCO   LONDON

CONTENTS

LIST OF ILLUSTRATIONS

INTRODUCTION

WHAT virtues do these stories possess that have kept them alive for so long a time? They have to some degree stimulated and nourished qualities of supreme worth in individual and social life. With the young the struggle against greed and falsehood and pride and cowardice is a very real one, and situations in which these homely, fundamental traits are involved are full of interest and seriousness. Again, to mature people the reward of well-doing and the punishment of evil conduct portrayed in these stories are apt to seem too realistic, too much also on the cut-and-dried pattern; but it is far different with children. They have a very concrete sense of right and wrong, and they demand a clear, explicit, tangible outcome for every sort of action. They must have concrete, living examples, with the appropriate outcome of each, set before them.

A modest, faithful child will be strengthened in his good qualities; while one lacking these will have them aroused, to some extent at any rate, by following Cinderella in her career. Arrogance and selfishness come to unhappy straits in this fancy world, and they are likely to fare the same in the real world; so it would be better to part company with them, and take up with gentleness and kindliness and faithfulness instead. And every one may be of some help to others if he be only of the right mind. The brother who thought himself faring badly with only a cat for a legacy learns betimes that even so small and apparently helpless a creature may be of much service when he is rightly disposed. A person might think little Thumb could accomplish nothing of value to any one, but he again teaches the child that all depends on the willingness to be of assistance, the good-heartedness, the fellow-feeling which one has for others.

In making this version anew the translator has endeavored to retain the characteristics of the style of the early chap-book versions, while evading the pompous, stilted language and Johnsonian phraseology so fashionable when they were first translated.

M. V. O'SHEA

UNIVERSITY OF WISCONSIN

The Tales of Mother Goose

—◦◦)◦(◦◦—

CINDERELLA, OR THE LITTLE GLASS SLIPPER

ONCE upon a time there was a gentleman who
married, for his second wife, the proudest and
most haughty woman that ever was seen. She
had two daughters of her own, who were, indeed,
exactly like her in all things. The gentleman
had also a young daughter, of rare goodness and
sweetness of temper, which she took from her
mother, who was the best creature in the world.

The wedding was scarcely over, when the stepmother's bad temper began to show itself. She
could not bear the goodness of this young girl, because it made her own daughters appear the more
odious. The stepmother gave her the meanest
work in the house to do; she had to scour the
dishes, tables, etc., and to scrub the floors and
clean out the bedrooms. The poor girl had to
sleep in the garret, upon a wretched straw bed,
while her sisters lay in fine rooms with inlaid
floors, upon beds of the very newest fashion, and
where they had looking-glasses so large that they

B

1

might see themselves at their full length. **The** poor girl bore all patiently, and dared not complain to her father, who would have scolded her if she had done so, for his wife governed him entirely.

When she had done her work, she used to go into the chimney corner, and sit down among the cinders, hence she was called Cinderwench. The younger sister of the two, who was not so rude and uncivil as the elder, called her Cinderella. However, Cinderella, in spite of her mean apparel, was a hundred times more handsome than her sisters, though they were always richly dressed.

It happened that the King's son gave a ball, and invited to it all persons of fashion. Our young misses were also invited, for they cut a very grand figure among the people of the country-side. They were highly delighted with the invitation, and wonderfully busy in choosing the gowns, petticoats, and head-dresses which might best become them. This made Cinderella's lot still harder, for it was she who ironed her sisters' linen and plaited their ruffles. They talked all day long of nothing but how they should be dressed.

" For my part," said the elder, " I will wear my red velvet suit with French trimmings."

" And I," said the younger, " shall wear my usual skirt; but then, to make amends for that

I will put on my gold-flowered mantle, and my diamond stomacher, which is far from being the most ordinary one in the world." They sent for the best hairdressers they could get to make up their hair in fashionable style, and bought patches for their cheeks. Cinderella was consulted in all these matters, for she had good taste. She advised them always for the best, and even offered her services to dress their hair, which they were very willing she should do.

As she was doing this, they said to her: —

" Cinderella, would you not be glad to go to the ball? "

" Young ladies," she said, " you only jeer at me; it is not for such as I am to go there."

" You are right," they replied; " people would laugh to see a Cinderwench at a ball."

Any one but Cinderella would have dressed their hair awry, but she was good-natured, and arranged it perfectly well. They were almost two days without eating, so much were they transported with joy. They broke above a dozen laces in trying to lace themselves tight, that they might have a fine, slender shape, and they were continually at their looking-glass.

At last the happy day came; they went to Court, and Cinderella followed them with her eyes as long as she could, and when she had lost sight of them, she fell a-crying.

Her godmother, who saw her all in tears, asked her what was the matter.

"I wish I could — I wish I could — " but she could not finish for sobbing.

Her godmother, who was a fairy, said to her, "You wish you could go to the ball; is it not so?"

"Alas, yes," said Cinderella, sighing.

"Well," said her godmother, "be but a good girl, and I will see that you go." Then she took her into her chamber, and said to her, "Run into the garden, and bring me a pumpkin."

Cinderella went at once to gather the finest she could get, and brought it to her godmother, not being able to imagine how this pumpkin could help her to go to the ball. Her godmother scooped out all the inside of it, leaving nothing but the rind. Then she struck it with her wand, and the pumpkin was instantly turned into a fine gilded coach.

She then went to look into the mouse-trap, where she found six mice, all alive. She ordered Cinderella to lift the trap-door, when, giving each mouse, as it went out, a little tap with her wand, it was that moment turned into a fine horse, and the six mice made a fine set of six horses of a beautiful mouse-colored, dapple gray.

Being at a loss for a coachman, Cinderella said, "I will go and see if there is not a rat in the rat-trap — we may make a coachman of him."

"You are right," replied her godmother; "go and look."

Cinderella brought the rat-trap to her, and in it there were three huge rats. The fairy chose the one which had the largest beard, and, having touched him with her wand, he was turned into a fat coachman with the finest mustache and whiskers ever seen.

After that, she said to her: —

"Go into the garden, and you will find six lizards behind the watering-pot; bring them to me."

She had no sooner done so than her godmother turned them into six footmen, who skipped up immediately behind the coach, with their liveries all trimmed with gold and silver, and they held on as if they had done nothing else their whole lives.

The fairy then said to Cinderella, "Well, you see here a carriage fit to go to the ball in; are you not pleased with it?"

"Oh, yes!" she cried; "but must I go as I am in these rags?"

Her godmother simply touched her with her wand, and, at the same moment, her clothes were turned into cloth of gold and silver, all decked with jewels. This done, she gave her a pair of the prettiest glass slippers in the whole world. Being thus attired, she got into the carriage, her godmother commanding her, above all things, not to stay till after midnight, and telling her, at the same time, that if she stayed one moment longer, the coach would be a pumpkin again, her horses mice, her coachman a rat, her footmen lizards, and her clothes would become just as they were before.

She promised her godmother she would not fail to leave the ball before midnight. She drove away, scarce able to contain herself for joy. The King's son, who was told that a great princess, whom nobody knew, was come, ran out to receive her. He gave her his hand as she alighted from the coach, and led her into the hall where the company were assembled. There was at once a profound silence; every one left off dancing, and the violins ceased to play, so attracted was every one by the singular beauties of the unknown new-comer. Nothing was then heard but a confused sound of voices saying: —

"Ha! how beautiful she is! Ha! how beautiful she is!"

The King himself, old as he was, could not keep his eyes off her, and he told the Queen under his breath that it was a long time since he had seen so beautiful and lovely a creature.

All the ladies were busy studying her clothes and head-dress, so that they might have theirs made next day after the same pattern, provided they could meet with such fine materials and able hands to make them.

The King's son conducted her to the seat of honor, and afterwards took her out to dance with him. She danced so very gracefully that they all admired her more and more. A fine collation was served, but the young Prince ate not a morsel, so intently was he occupied with her.

She went and sat down beside her sisters, showing them a thousand civilities, and giving them among other things part of the oranges and citrons with which the Prince had regaled her. This very much surprised them, for they had not been presented to her.

Cinderella heard the clock strike a quarter to twelve. She at once made her adieus to the company and hastened away as fast as she could.

As soon as she got home, she ran to find her godmother, and, after having thanked her, she said she much wished she might go to the ball the next day, because the King's son had asked her to do so. As she was eagerly telling her godmother all that happened at the ball, her two sisters knocked at the door; Cinderella opened it. "How long you have stayed!" said she, yawning, rubbing her eyes, and stretching herself as if she had been just awakened. She had not, however, had any desire to sleep since they went from home.

"If you had been at the ball," said one of her sisters, "you would not have been tired with it. There came thither the finest princess, the most beautiful ever was seen with mortal eyes. She showed us a thousand civilities, and gave us oranges and citrons."

Cinderella did not show any pleasure at this. Indeed, she asked them the name of the princess; but they told her they did not know it, and that the King's son was very much concerned, and would give all the world to know who she was. At this Cinderella, smiling, replied : —

"Was she then so very beautiful? How fortunate you have been! Could I not see her? Ah! dear Miss Charlotte, do lend me your yellow suit of clothes which you wear every day."

"Ay, to be sure!" cried Miss Charlotte; "lend my clothes to such a dirty Cinderwench as thou art! I should be out of my mind to do so."

Cinderella, indeed, expected such an answer and was very glad of the refusal; for she would have been sadly troubled if her sister had lent her what she jestingly asked for. The next day the two sisters went to the ball, and so did Cinderella, but dressed more magnificently than before. The King's son was always by her side, and his pretty speeches to her never ceased. These by no means annoyed the young lady. Indeed, she quite forgot her godmother's orders to her, so that she heard the clock begin to strike twelve when she thought it could not be more than eleven.   She then rose up and fled, as nimble as a deer.   The Prince followed, but could not overtake her.   She left behind one of her glass slippers, which the Prince took up most carefully.   She got home, but quite out of breath, without her carriage, and in her old clothes, having nothing left her of all her finery but one of the little slippers, fellow to the one she had dropped.   The guards at the palace gate were asked if they had not seen a princess go out, and they replied they had seen nobody go out but a young girl, very meanly dressed, and who had more• the air of a poor country girl than of a young lady.

When the two sisters returned from the ball, Cinderella asked them if they had had a pleasant time, and if the fine lady had been there.   They told her, yes; but that she hurried away the moment it struck twelve, and with so much haste that she dropped one of her little glass slippers, the prettiest in the world, which the King's son had taken up.   They said, further, that he had done nothing but look at her all the time, and that most certainly he was very much in love with the beautiful owner of the glass slipper.

What they said was true; for a few days after the King's son caused it to be proclaimed, by sound of trumpet, that he would marry her whose

foot this slipper would fit exactly. They began
to try it on the princesses, then on the duchesses,
and then on all the ladies of the Court; but in
vain. It was brought to the two sisters, who
did all they possibly could to thrust a foot into
the slipper, but they could not succeed. Cinderella, who saw this, and knew her slipper, said
to them, laughing : —

"Let me see if it will not fit me."

Her sisters burst out a-laughing, and began to
banter her. The gentleman who was sent to try
the slipper looked earnestly at Cinderella, and,
finding her very handsome, said it was but just
that she should try, and that he had orders to let
every lady try it on.

He obliged Cinderella to sit down, and, putting
the slipper to her little foot, he found it went on
very easily, and fitted her as if it had been made
of wax. The astonishment of her two sisters was
great, but it was still greater when Cinderella
pulled out of her pocket the other slipper and
put it on her foot. Thereupon, in came her
godmother, who, having touched Cinderella's
clothes with her wand, made them more magnificent than those she had worn before.

And now her two sisters found her to be that
beautiful lady they had seen at the ball. They
threw themselves at her feet to beg pardon for
all their ill treatment of her. Cinderella took

"IT WENT ON VERY EASILY."

them up, and, as she embraced them, said that she forgave them with all her heart, and begged them to love her always.

She was conducted to the young Prince, dressed as she was. He thought her more charming than ever, and, a few days after, married her. Cinderella, who was as good as she was beautiful, gave her two sisters a home in the palace, and that very same day married them to two great lords of the Court.

THE SLEEPING BEAUTY IN THE WOODS

ONCE upon a time there was a king and a queen, who were very sorry that they had no children, — so sorry that it cannot be told.

At last, however, the Queen had a daughter. There was a very fine christening; and the Princess had for her godmothers all the fairies they could find in the whole kingdom (there were seven of them), so that every one of them might confer a gift upon her, as was the custom of fairies in those days. By this means the Princess had all the perfections imaginable.

After the christening was over, the company returned to the King's palace, where was prepared a great feast for the fairies. There was placed before every one of them a magnificent cover with a case of massive gold, wherein were a spoon, and a knife and fork, all of pure gold set with diamonds and rubies. But as they were all sitting down at table they saw a very old fairy come into the hall. She had not been invited, because for more than fifty years she had not been out of a certain tower, and she was believed to be either dead or enchanted.

The King ordered her a cover, but he could not give her a case of gold as the others had, because seven only had been made for the seven fairies. The old fairy fancied she was slighted, and muttered threats between her teeth. One of the young fairies who sat near heard her, and, judging that she might give the little Princess some unlucky gift, hid herself behind the curtains as soon as they left the table. She hoped that she might speak last and undo as much as she could the evil which the old fairy might do.

In the meanwhile all the fairies began to give their gifts to the Princess. The youngest gave her for her gift that she should be the most beautiful person in the world; the next, that she should have the wit of an angel; the third, that she should be able to do everything she did gracefully; the fourth, that she should dance perfectly; the fifth, that she should sing like a nightingale; and the sixth, that she should play all kinds of musical instruments to the fullest perfection.

The old fairy's turn coming next, her head shaking more with spite than with age, she said that the Princess should pierce her hand with a spindle and die of the wound. This terrible gift made the whole company tremble, and everybody fell a-crying.

At this very instant the young fairy came from

behind the curtains and said these words in a loud voice : —

" Assure yourselves, O King and Queen, that your daughter shall not die of this disaster. It is true, I have no power to undo entirely what my elder has done. The Princess shall indeed pierce her hand with a spindle ; but, instead of dying, she shall only fall into a deep sleep, which shall last a hundred years, at the end of which a king's son shall come and awake her."

The King, to avoid the misfortune foretold by the old fairy, issued orders forbidding any one, on pain of death, to spin with a distaff and spindle, or to have a spindle in his house. About fifteen or sixteen years after, the King and Queen being absent at one of their country villas, the young Princess was one day running up and down the palace ; she went from room to room, and at last she came into a little garret on the top of the tower, where a good old woman, alone, was spinning with her spindle. This good woman had never heard of the King's orders against spindles.

" What are you doing there, my good woman ? " said the Princess.

" I am spinning, my pretty child," said the old woman, who did not know who the Princess was.

" Ha ! " said the Princess, " this is very pretty ; how do you do it ? Give it to me. Let me see if I can do it."

She had no sooner taken it into her hand **than,** either because she was too quick and heedless, **or** because the decree of the fairy had so ordained, it ran into her hand, and she fell down in **a** swoon.

The good old woman, not knowing what to do, cried out for help. People came in from every quarter; they threw water upon the face of the Princess, unlaced her, struck her on the palms of her hands, and rubbed her temples with cologne water; but nothing would bring her to herself.

Then the King, who came up at hearing the noise, remembered what the fairies had foretold. He knew very well that this must come to pass, since the fairies had foretold it, and he caused the Princess to be carried into the finest room in his palace, and to be laid upon a bed all embroidered with gold and silver. One would have taken her for a little angel, she was so beautiful; for her swooning had not dimmed the brightness of her complexion: her cheeks were carnation, and her lips coral. It is true her eyes were shut, but she was heard to breathe softly, which satisfied those about her that she was not dead.

The King gave orders that they should let her sleep quietly till the time came for her to awake. The good fairy who had saved her life by condemning her to sleep a hundred years **was in the** kingdom of Matakin, twelve thousand leagues off,

"LET ME SEE IF I CAN DO IT."

when this accident befell the Princess; but she was instantly informed of it by a little dwarf, who had seven-leagued boots, that is, boots with which he could stride over seven leagues of ground at once. The fairy started off at once, and arrived, about an hour later, in a fiery chariot drawn by dragons.

The King handed her out of the chariot, and she approved everything he had done; but as she had very great foresight, she thought that when the Princess should awake she might not know what to do with herself, if she was all alone in this old palace. This was what she did: she touched with her wand everything in the palace (except the King and Queen),—governesses, maids of honor, ladies of the bedchamber, gentlemen, officers, stewards, cooks, undercooks, kitchen maids, guards with their porters, pages, and footmen; she likewise touched all the horses which were in the stables, the cart horses, the hunters and the saddle horses, the grooms, the great dogs in the outward court, and little Mopsey, too, the Princess's spaniel, which was lying on the bed.

As soon as she touched them they all fell asleep, not to awake again until their mistress did, that they might be ready to wait upon her when she wanted them. The very spits at the fire, as full as they could hold of partridges and pheasants, fell asleep, and the fire itself as well.

All this was done in a moment.   Fairies are not long in doing their work.

And now the King and Queen, having kissed their dear child without waking her, went out of the palace and sent forth orders that nobody should come near it.

These orders were not necessary; for in a quarter of an hour's time there grew up all round about the park such a vast number of trees, great and small, bushes and brambles, twining one within another, that neither man nor beast could pass through; so that nothing could be seen but the very top of the towers of the palace; and that, too, only from afar off.   Every one knew that this also was the work of the fairy in order that while the Princess slept she should have nothing to fear from curious people.

After a hundred years the son of the King then reigning, who was of another family from that of the sleeping Princess, was a-hunting on that side of the country, and he asked what those towers were which he saw in the middle of a great thick wood.   Every one answered according as they had heard.   Some said that it was an old haunted castle, others that all the witches of the country held their midnight revels there, but the common opinion was that it was an ogre's dwelling, and that he carried to it all the little children he could catch, so as to eat them up at his leisure, without any one being able to follow him, for he alone had the power to make his way through the wood.

The Prince did not know what to believe, and presently a very aged countryman spake to him thus : —

" May it please your royal Highness, more than fifty years since I heard from my father that there was then in this castle the most beautiful princess that was ever seen; that she must sleep there a hundred years, and that she should be waked by a king's son, for whom she was reserved."

The young Prince on hearing this was all on fire. He thought, without weighing the matter, that he could put an end to this rare adventure; and, pushed on by love and the desire of glory, resolved at once to look into it.

As soon as he began to get near to the wood, all the great trees, the bushes, and brambles gave way of themselves to let him pass through. He walked up to the castle which he saw at the end of a large avenue; and you can imagine he was a good deal surprised when he saw none of his people following him, because the trees closed again as soon as he had passed through them. However, he did not cease from continuing his way; a young prince in search of glory is ever valiant.

He came into a spacious outer court, and what he saw was enough to freeze him with horror. A frightful silence reigned over all, the image of death was everywhere, and there was nothing to be seen but what seemed to be the outstretched bodies of dead men and animals. He, however, very well knew, by the ruby faces and pimpled noses of the porters, that they were only asleep; and their goblets, wherein still remained some drops of wine, showed plainly that they had fallen asleep while drinking their wine.

He then crossed a court paved with marble, went up the stairs, and came into the guard chamber, where guards were standing in their ranks, with their muskets upon their shoulders, and snoring with all their might. He went through several rooms full of gentlemen and ladies, some standing and others sitting, but all were asleep. He came into a gilded chamber, where he saw upon a bed, the curtains of which were all open, the most beautiful sight ever beheld — a princess who appeared to be about fifteen or sixteen years of age, and whose bright and resplendent beauty had something divine in it. He approached with trembling and admiration, and fell down upon his knees before her.

Then, as the end of the enchantment was come, the Princess awoke, and looking on him with eyes more tender than could have been expected at first sight, said : —

"Is it you, my Prince? You have waited a long while."

The Prince, charmed with these words, and much more with the manner in which they were spoken, knew not how to show his joy and gratitude; he assured her that he loved her better than he did himself. Their discourse was not very connected, but they were the better pleased, for where there is much love there is little eloquence. He was more at a loss than she, and we need not wonder at it; she had had time to think of what to say to him; for it is evident (though history says nothing of it) that the good fairy, during so long a sleep, had given her very pleasant dreams. In short, they talked together for four hours, and then they said not half they had to say.

In the meanwhile all the palace had woke up with the Princess; every one thought upon his own business, and as they were not in love, they were ready to die of hunger. The lady of honor, being as sharp set as the other folks, grew very impatient, and told the Princess aloud that the meal was served. The Prince helped the Princess to rise. She was entirely and very magnificently dressed; but his royal Highness took care not to tell her that she was dressed like his great-grandmother, and had a high collar. She looked not a bit the less charming and beautiful for all that.

They went into the great mirrored hall, where they supped, and were served by the officers of the Princess's household. The violins and hautboys played old tunes, but they were excellent, though they had not been played for a hundred years; and after supper, without losing any time, the lord almoner married them in the chapel of the castle.   They had but very little sleep — the Princess scarcely needed any; and the Prince left her next morning to return into the city, where his father was greatly troubled about him.

The Prince told him that he lost his way in the forest as he was hunting, and that he had slept in the cottage of a charcoal-burner, who gave him cheese and brown bread.

The King, his father, who was a good man, believed him; but his mother could not be persuaded that it was true; and seeing that he went almost every day a-hunting, and that he always had some excuse ready for so doing, though he had been out three or four nights together, she began to suspect that he was married; for he lived thus with the Princess above two whole years, during which they had two children, the elder, a daughter, was named Dawn, and the younger, a son, they called Day, because he was a great deal handsomer than his sister.

The Queen spoke several times to her son, to learn after what manner he was passing his time, and told him that in this he ought in duty to satisfy her.   But he never dared to trust her with his secret; he feared her, though he loved her, for she was of the race of the Ogres, and the King married her for her vast riches alone. It was even whispered about the Court that she had Ogreish inclinations, and that, whenever she saw little children passing by, she had all the difficulty in the world to prevent herself from falling upon them. And so the Prince would never tell her one word.

But when the King was dead, which happened about two years afterward, and he saw himself lord and master, he openly declared his marriage; and he went in great state to conduct his Queen to the palace. They made a magnificent entry into the capital city, she riding between her two children.

Soon after, the King made war on Emperor Cantalabutte, his neighbor. He left the government of the kingdom to the Queen, his mother, and earnestly commended his wife and children to her care. He was obliged to carry on the war all the summer, and as soon as he left, the Queen-mother sent her daughter-in-law and her children to a country house among the woods, that she might with the more ease gratify her horrible longing. Some few days afterward she went thither herself, and said to her head cook:—

"I intend to eat little Dawn for my dinner to-morrow."

"O! madam!" cried the head cook.

" I will have it so," replied the Queen (and this she spoke in the tone of an Ogress who had a strong desire to eat fresh meat), "and will eat her with a sharp sauce."

The poor man, knowing very well that he must not play tricks with Ogresses, took his great knife and went up into little Dawn's chamber. She was then nearly four years old, and came up to him, jumping and laughing, to put her arms round his neck, and ask him for some sugar-candy. Upon which he began to weep, the great knife fell out of his hand, and he went into the back yard and killed a little lamb, and dressed it with such good sauce that his mistress assured him she had never eaten anything so good in her life. He had at the same time taken up little Dawn and carried her to his wife, to conceal her in his lodging at the end of the courtyard.

Eight days afterwards the wicked Queen said to the chief cook, "I will sup upon little Day."

He answered not a word, being resolved to cheat her again as he had done before. He went to find little Day, and saw him with a foil in his hand, with which he was fencing with a great monkey: the child was then only three years of age. He took him up in his arms and carried him to his wife, that she might conceal him in her chamber along with his sister, and instead of little Day he served up a young and very

tender kid, which the Ogress found to be wonderfully good.

All had gone well up to now; but one evening
this wicked Queen said to her chief cook : —

"I will eat the Queen with the same sauce I
had with her children."

Now the poor chief cook was in despair and
could not imagine how to deceive her again.
The young Queen was over twenty years old,
not reckoning the hundred years she had been
asleep; and how to find something to take her
place greatly puzzled him. He then decided, to
save his own life, to cut the Queen's throat; and
going up into her chamber, with intent to do it
at once, he put himself into as great fury as he
possibly could, and came into the young Queen's
room with his dagger in his hand. He would
not, however, deceive her, but told her, with a
great deal of respect, the orders he had received
from the Queen-mother.

"Do it; do it," she said, stretching out her
neck. "Carry out your orders, and then I shall
go and see my children, my poor children, whom
I loved so much and so tenderly."

For she thought them dead, since they had
been taken away without her knowledge.

"No, no, madam," cried the poor chief cook,
all in tears; "you shall not die, and you shall see
your children again at once. But then you must

go home with me to my lodgings, where I have
concealed them, and I will deceive the Queen
once more, by giving her a young hind in your
stead."

Upon this he forthwith conducted her to his
room, where, leaving her to embrace her children,
and cry along with them, he went and dressed a
young hind, which the Queen had for her supper,
and devoured with as much appetite as if it had
been the young Queen. She was now well satisfied with her cruel deeds, and she invented a story
to tell the King on his return, of how the Queen
his wife and her two children had been devoured
by mad wolves.

One evening, as she was, according to her
custom, rambling round about the courts and
yards of the palace to see if she could smell any
fresh meat, she heard, in a room on the ground
floor, little Day crying, for his mamma was going
to whip him, because he had been naughty; and
she heard, at the same time, little Dawn begging
mercy for her brother.

The Ogress knew the voice of the Queen and
her children at once, and being furious at having
been thus deceived, she gave orders (in a most
horrible voice which made everybody tremble)
that, next morning by break of day, they should
bring into the middle of the great court a large
tub filled with toads, vipers, snakes, and all sorts

of serpents, in order to have the Queen and her children, the chief cook, his wife and maid, thrown into it, all of whom were to be brought thither with their hands tied behind them.

They were brought out accordingly, and the executioners were just going to throw them into the tub, when the King, who was not so soon expected, entered the court on horseback and asked, with the utmost astonishment, what was the meaning of that horrible spectacle.

No one dared to tell him, when the Ogress, all enraged to see what had happened, threw herself head foremost into the tub, and was instantly devoured by the ugly creatures she had ordered to be thrown into it to kill the others. The King was of course very sorry, for she was his mother; but he soon comforted himself with his beautiful wife and his pretty children.

LITTLE THUMB

ONCE upon a time there was a fagot-maker and his wife, who had seven children, all boys. The eldest was but ten years old, and the youngest only seven.

They were very poor, and their seven children were a great source of trouble to them because not one of them was able to earn his bread. What gave them yet more uneasiness was that the youngest was very delicate, and scarce ever spoke a word, which made people take for stupidity that which was a sign of good sense. He was very little, and when born he was no bigger than one's thumb; hence he was called Little Thumb.

The poor child was the 'drudge of the household, and was always in the wrong. He was, however, the most bright and discreet of all the brothers; and if he spoke little, he heard and thought the more.

There came a very bad year, and the famine was so great that these poor people resolved to rid themselves of their children. One evening, when they were in bed, and the fagot-maker was sitting with his wife at the fire, he said to her, with his heart ready to burst with grief : —

"You see plainly that we no longer can give our children food, and I cannot bear to see them die of hunger before my eyes; I am resolved to lose them in the wood to-morrow, which may very easily be done, for, while they amuse themselves in tying up fagots, we have only to run away and leave them without their seeing us."

"Ah!" cried out his wife, "could you really take the children and lose them?"

In vain did her husband represent to her their great poverty; she would not consent to it. She was poor, but she was their mother.

However, having considered what a grief it would be to her to see them die of hunger, she consented, and went weeping to bed.

Little Thumb heard all they had said; for, hearing that they were talking business, he got up softly and slipped under his father's seat, so as to hear without being seen. He went to bed again, but did not sleep a wink all the rest of the night, thinking of what he had to do. He got up early in the morning, and went to the brookside, where he filled his pockets full of small white pebbles, and then returned home. They all went out, but Little Thumb never told his brothers a word of what he knew.

They went into a very thick forest, where they

"Slipped under his Father's Seat."

31

could not see one another at ten paces apart.
The fagot-maker began to cut wood, and the children to gather up sticks to make fagots. Their
father and mother, seeing them busy at their
work, got away from them unbeknown and then
all at once ran as fast as they could through a
winding by-path.

When the children found they were alone, they
began to cry with all their might. Little Thumb
let them cry on, knowing very well how to get
home again; for, as he came, he had dropped
the little white pebbles he had in his pockets all
along the way. Then he said to them, "Do not
be afraid, my brothers, — father and mother have
left us here, but I will lead you home again; only
follow me."

They followed, and he brought them home by
the very same way they had come into the forest.
They dared not go in at first, but stood outside
the door to listen to what their father and mother
were saying.

The very moment the fagot-maker and his wife
reached home the lord of the manor sent them
ten crowns, which he had long owed them, and
which they never hoped to see. This gave them
new life, for the poor people were dying of
hunger. The fagot-maker sent his wife to the
butcher's at once. As it was a long while since
they had eaten, she bought thrice as much meat

as was needed for supper for two people. When they had eaten, the woman said : —

"Alas! where are our poor children now? They would make a good feast of what we have left here; it was you, William, who wished to lose them. I told you we should repent of it. What are they now doing in the forest? Alas! perhaps the wolves have already eaten them up; you are very inhuman thus to have lost your children."

The fagot-maker grew at last quite out of patience, for she repeated twenty times that he would repent of it, and that she was in the right. He threatened to beat her if she did not hold her tongue. The fagot-maker was, perhaps, more sorry than his wife, but she teased him so he could not endure it. She wept bitterly, saying : —

"Alas! where are my children now, my poor children?"

She said this once so very loud that the children, who were at the door, heard her and cried out all together : —

"Here we are! Here we are!"

She ran immediately to let them in, and said as she embraced them : —

"How happy I am to see you again, my dear children; you are very tired and very hungry, and, my poor Peter, you are covered with mud. Come in and let me clean you."

D

Peter was her eldest son, whom she loved **more** than all the rest, because he was red haired, **as** she was herself.

They sat down to table, and ate with an appetite which pleased both father and mother, to whom they told how frightened they were in the forest, nearly all speaking at once. The good folk were delighted to see their children once more, and this joy continued while the ten crowns lasted. But when the money was all spent, they · fell again into their former uneasiness, and resolved to lose their children again. And, that they might be the surer of doing it, they determined to take them much farther than before.

They could not talk of this so secretly but they were overheard by Little Thumb, who laid his plans to get out of the difficulty as he had done before; but, though he got up very early to go and pick up some little pebbles, he could not, for he found the house-door double-locked. He did not know what to do. Their father had given each of them a piece of bread for their breakfast. He reflected that he might make use of the bread instead of the pebbles, by throwing crumbs all along the way they should pass, and so he stuffed it in his pocket. Their father and mother led them into the thickest and most obscure part of the forest, and then, stealing away into a by-path, left them there. Little Thumb was not **very** much worried about it, for he thought he could easily find the way again by means of his bread, which he had scattered all along as he came; but he was very much surprised when he could not find a single crumb: the birds had come and eaten them all.

They were now in great trouble; for the more they wandered, the deeper they went into the forest. Night now fell, and there arose a high wind, which filled them with fear. They fancied they heard on every side the howling of wolves coming to devour them. They scarce dared to speak or turn their heads. Then it rained very hard, which wetted them to the skin. Their feet slipped at every step, and they fell into the mud, covering their hands with it so that they knew not what to do with them.

Little Thumb climbed up to the top of a tree, to see if he could discover anything. Looking on every side, he saw at last a glimmering light, like that of a candle, but a long way beyond the forest. He came down, and, when upon the ground, he he could see it no more, which grieved him sadly. However, having walked for some time with his brothers toward that side on which he had seen the light, he discovered it again as he came out of the wood.

They arrived at last at the house where this candle was, not without many frights; for very

often they lost sight of it, which happened every
time they came into a hollow. They knocked at
the door, and a good woman came and opened it.

She asked them what they wanted. Little
Thumb told her they were poor children who
were lost in the forest, and desired to lodge there
for charity's sake. The woman, seeing them all
so very pretty, began to weep and said to them:
"Alas! poor babies, where do you come from?
Do you know that this house belongs to a cruel
Ogre who eats little children?"

"Alas! dear madam," answered Little Thumb
(who, with his brothers, was trembling in every
limb), "what shall we do? The wolves of the
forest surely will devour us to-night if you refuse
us shelter in your house; and so we would rather
the gentleman should eat us. Perhaps he may
take pity upon us if you will be pleased to ask
him to do so."

The Ogre's wife, who believed she could hide
them from her husband till morning, let them
come in, and took them to warm themselves at
a very good fire; for there was a whole sheep
roasting for the Ogre's supper.

As they began to warm themselves they heard
three or four great raps at the door; this was the
Ogre, who was come home. His wife quickly hid
them under the bed and went to open the door.
The Ogre at once asked if supper was ready and

the wine drawn, and then sat himself down to
table.   The sheep was as yet all raw, but he liked
it the better for that.   He sniffed about to the
right and left, saying : —

" I smell fresh meat."

" What you smell," said his wife, " must be the
calf which I have just now killed and flayed."

" I smell fresh meat, I tell you once more,"
replied the Ogre, looking crossly at his wife, " and
there is something here which I do not understand."

As he spoke these words he got up from the
table and went straight to the bed.

. " Ah ! " said he, "that is how you would cheat
me ; I know not why I do not eat you, too ; it is
well for you that you are tough.   Here is game,
which comes very luckily to entertain three Ogres
of my acquaintance who are to pay me a visit in
a day or two."

He dragged them out from under the bed, one
by one.   The poor children fell upon their knees
and begged his pardon, but they had to do with
one of the most cruel of Ogres, who, far from
having any pity on them, was already devouring
them in his mind, and told his wife they would be
delicate eating when she had made a good sauce.

He then took a great knife, and, coming up to
these poor children, sharpened it upon a great
whetstone which he held in his left hand.   He

had already taken hold of one of them when his wife said to him: —

"What need you do it now? Will you not have time enough to-morrow?"

"Hold your prating," said the Ogre; "they will eat the tenderer."

"But you have so much meat already," replied his wife; "here are a calf, two sheep, and half a pig."

"That is true," said the Ogre; "give them a good supper that they may not grow thin, and put them to bed."

The good woman was overjoyed at this, and gave them a good supper; but they were so much afraid that they could not eat. As for the Ogre, he sat down again to drink, being highly pleased that he had the wherewithal to treat his friends. He drank a dozen glasses more than ordinary, which got up into his head and obliged him to go to bed.

The Ogre had seven daughters, who were still little children. These young Ogresses had all of them very fine complexions; but they all had little gray eyes, quite round, hooked noses, a very large mouth, and very long, sharp teeth, set far apart. They were not as yet wicked, but they promised well to be, for they had already bitten little children.

They had been put to bed early, all seven in

one bed, with every one a crown of gold upon
her head. There was in the same chamber a
bed of the like size, and the Ogre's wife put the
seven little boys into this bed, after which she
went to bed herself.

Little Thumb, who had observed that the
Ogre's daughters had crowns of gold upon their
heads, and was afraid lest the Ogre should repent
his not killing them that evening, got up about
midnight, and, taking his brothers' bonnets and
his own, went very softly and put them upon the
heads of the seven little Ogresses, after having
taken off their crowns of gold, which he put
upon his own head and his brothers', so that the
Ogre might take them for his daughters, and his
daughters for the little boys whom he wanted to
kill.

Things turned out just as he had thought; for
the Ogre, waking about midnight, regretted that
he had deferred till morning to do that which he
might have done overnight, and jumped quickly
out of bed, taking his great knife.

"Let us see," said he, "how our little rogues
do, and not make two jobs of the matter."

He then went up, groping all the way, into
his daughters' chamber; and, coming to the bed
where the little boys lay, and who were all fast
asleep, except Little Thumb, who was terribly
afraid when he found the Ogre fumbling about

his head, as he had done about his brothers', he felt the golden crowns, and said : —

" I should have made a fine piece of work of it, truly ; it is clear I drank too much last night."

Then he went to the bed where the girls lay, and, having found the boys' little bonnets : —

" Ah ! " said he, " my merry lads, are you there ? Let us work boldly."

And saying these words, without more ado, he cruelly murdered all his seven daughters. Well pleased with what he had done, he went to bed again.

So soon as Little Thumb heard the Ogre snore, he waked his brothers, and bade them put on their clothes quickly and follow him. They stole softly into the garden and got over the wall. They ran about all night, trembling all the while, without knowing which way they went.

The Ogre, when he woke, said to his wife : " Go upstairs and dress those young rascals who came here last night." The Ogress was very much surprised at this goodness of her husband, not dreaming after what manner she should dress them ; but, thinking that he had ordered her to go up and put on their clothes, she went, and was horrified when she perceived her seven daughters all dead.

She began by fainting away, as was only natural in such a case. The Ogre, fearing his wife was

too long in doing what he had ordered, went up
himself to help her. He was no less amazed than
his wife at this frightful spectacle.

"Ah! what have I done?" cried he. "The
wretches shall pay for it, and that instantly."

He threw a pitcher of water upon his wife's
face, and having brought her to herself, "Give
me quickly," cried he, "my seven-leagued boots,
that I may go and catch them."

He went out into the country, and, after running in all directions, he came at last into the
very road where the poor children were, and not
above a hundred paces from their father's house.
They espied the Ogre, who went at one step from
mountain to mountain, and over rivers as easily
as the narrowest brooks. Little Thumb, seeing
a hollow rock near the place where they were,
hid his brothers in it, and crowded into it himself, watching always what would become of the
Ogre.

The Ogre, who found himself tired with his
long and fruitless journey (for these boots of
seven leagues greatly taxed the wearer), had a
great mind to rest himself, and, by chance, went
to sit down upon the rock in which the little
boys had hidden themselves. As he was worn out
with fatigue, he fell asleep, and, after reposing
himself some time, began to snore so frightfully
that the poor children were no less afraid of him

than when he held up his great knife and was
going to take their lives.   Little Thumb was not
so much frightened as his brothers, and told them
that they should run away at once toward home
while the Ogre was asleep so soundly, and that
they need not be in any trouble about him.   They
took his advice, and got home quickly.

Little Thumb then went close to the Ogre,
pulled off his boots gently, and put them on his
own legs.   The boots were very long and large,
but as they were fairy boots, they had the gift of
becoming big or little, according to the legs of
those who wore them; so that they fitted his feet
and legs as well as if they had been made for him.
He went straight to the Ogre's house, where he
saw his wife crying bitterly for the loss of her
murdered daughters.

"Your husband," said Little Thumb, "is in
very great danger, for he has been taken by a
gang of thieves, who have sworn to kill him if he
does not give them all his gold and silver.   At
the very moment they held their daggers at his
throat he perceived me and begged me to come
and tell you the condition he was in, and to say
that you should give me all he has of value, without retaining any one thing; for otherwise they
will kill him without mercy.   As his case is very
pressing, he desired me to make use of his seven-
leagued boots, which you see I have on, so that I

might make the more haste and that I might show
you that I do not impose upon you."

The good woman, being greatly frightened, gave
him all she had; for this Ogre was a very good
husband, though he ate up little children. Little
Thumb, having thus got all the Ogre's money,
came home to his father's house, where he was
received with abundance of joy.

There are many people who do not agree in re-
gard to this act of Little Thumb's, and pretend that
he never robbed the Ogre at all, and that he only
thought he might very justly take off his seven-
leagued boots because he made no other use of
them but to run after little children. These folks
affirm that they are very well assured of this, because they have drunk and eaten often at the
fagot-maker's house. They declare that when
Little Thumb had taken off the Ogre's boots he
went to Court, where he was informed that they
were very much in trouble about a certain army,
which was two hundred leagues off, and anxious
as to the success of a battle. He went, they say,
to the King and told him that if he desired it,
he would bring him news from the army before
night.

The King promised him a great sum of money
if he succeeded. Little Thumb returned that very
same night with the news; and, this first expedi-
tion causing him to be known, he earned as much

as he wished, for the King paid him very well for carrying his orders to the army. Many ladies employed him also to carry messages, from which he made much money. After having for some time carried on the business of a messenger and gained thereby great wealth, he went home to his father, and it is impossible to express the joy of his family. He placed them all in comfortable circumstances, bought places for his father and brothers, and by that means settled them very handsomely in the world, while he successfully continued to make his own way.

THE MASTER CAT, OR PUSS IN BOOTS

ONCE upon a time there was a miller who left no more riches to the three sons he had than his mill, his ass, and his cat. The division was soon made. Neither the lawyer nor the attorney was sent for. They would soon have eaten up all the poor property. The eldest had the mill, the second the ass, and the youngest nothing but the cat.

The youngest, as we can understand, was quite unhappy at having so poor a share.

"My brothers," said he, "may get their living handsomely enough by joining their stocks together; but, for my part, when I have eaten up my cat, and made me a muff of his skin, I must die of hunger."

The Cat, who heard all this, without appearing to take any notice, said to him with a grave and serious air: —

"Do not thus afflict yourself, my master; you have nothing else to do but to give me a bag, and get a pair of boots made for me, that I may scamper through the brambles, and you shall see that you have not so poor a portion in me as you think."

Though the Cat's master did not think much of what he said, he had seen him play such cunning tricks to catch rats and mice — hanging himself by the heels, or hiding himself in the meal, to make believe he was dead — that he did not altogether despair of his helping him in his misery. When the Cat had what he asked for, he booted himself very gallantly, and putting his bag about his neck, he held the strings of it in his two forepaws, and went into a warren where was a great number of rabbits. He put bran and sow-thistle into his bag, and, stretching out at length, as if he were dead, he waited for some young rabbits, not yet acquainted with the deceits of the world, to come and rummage his bag for what he had put into it.

Scarcely was he settled but he had what he wanted. A rash and foolish young rabbit jumped into his bag, and Monsieur Puss, immediately drawing close the strings, took him and killed him at once. Proud of his prey, he went with it to the palace, and asked to speak with the King. He was shown upstairs into his Majesty's apartment, and, making a low bow to the King, he said : —

"I have brought you, sire, a rabbit which my noble Lord, the Master of Carabas " (for that was the title which Puss was pleased to give his master) "has commanded me to present to your Majesty from him."

"Tell thy master," said the King, "that I thank him, and that I am pleased with his gift."

Another time he went and hid himself among some standing corn, still holding his bag open; and when a brace of partridges ran into it, he drew the strings, and so caught them both. He then went and made a present of these to the King, as he had done before of the rabbit which he took in the warren. The King, in like manner, received the partridges with great pleasure, and ordered his servants to reward him.

The Cat continued for two or three months thus to carry his Majesty, from time to time, some of his master's game. One day when he knew that the King was to take the air along the riverside, with his daughter, the most beautiful princess in the world, he said to his master: —

"If you will follow my advice, your fortune is made. You have nothing else to do but go and bathe in the river, just at the spot I shall show you, and leave the rest to me."

The Marquis of Carabas did what the Cat advised him to, without knowing what could be the use of doing it. While he was bathing, the King passed by, and the Cat cried out with all his might: —

" Help ! help ! My Lord the Marquis of Carabas is drowning !"

At this noise the King put his head out of the coach window, and seeing the Cat who had so often brought him game, he commanded his guards to run immediately to the assistance of his Lordship the Marquis of Carabas.

While they were drawing the poor Marquis out of the river, the Cat came up to the coach and told the King that, while his master was bathing, there came by some rogues, who ran off with his clothes, though he had cried out, " Thieves ! thieves !" several times, as loud as he could. The cunning Cat had hidden the clothes under a great stone. The King immediately commanded the officers of his wardrobe to run and fetch one of his best suits for the Lord Marquis of Carabas.

The King was extremely polite to him, and as the fine clothes he had given him set off his good looks (for he was well made and handsome), the King's daughter found him very much to her liking, and the Marquis of Carabas had no sooner cast two or three respectful and somewhat tender glances than she fell in love with him to distraction. The King would have him come into the coach and take part in the airing. The Cat, overjoyed to see his plan begin to succeed, marched on before, and, meeting with some countrymen, who were mowing a meadow, he said to them : —

"The Marquis of Carabas is drowning!"

"Good people, you who are mowing, if you do not tell the King that the meadow you mow belongs to my Lord Marquis of Carabas, you shall be chopped as small as herbs for the pot."

The King did not fail to ask the mowers to whom the meadow they were mowing belonged.

"To my Lord Marquis of Carabas," answered . they all together, for the Cat's threat had made them afraid.

"You have a good property there," said the King to the Marquis of Carabas.

"You see, sire," said the Marquis, "this is a meadow which never fails to yield a plentiful harvest every year."

The Master Cat, who went still on before, met with some reapers, and said to them: —

"Good people, you who are reaping, if you do not say that all this corn belongs to the Marquis of Carabas, you shall be chopped as small as herbs for the pot."

The King, who passed by a moment after, wished to know to whom belonged all that corn, which he then saw.

"To my Lord Marquis of Carabas," replied the reapers, and the King was very well pleased with it, as well as the Marquis, whom he congratulated thereupon. The Master Cat, who went always before, said the same thing to all he met, and the

King was astonished at the vast estates of my Lord Marquis of Carabas.

Monsieur Puss came at last to a stately castle, the master of which was an Ogre, the richest ever known; for all the lands which the King had then passed through belonged to this castle. The Cat, who had taken care to inform himself who this Ogre was and what he could do, asked to speak with him, saying he could not pass so near his castle without having the honor of paying his respects to him.

The Ogre received him as civilly as an Ogre could do, and made him sit down.

" I have been assured," said the Cat, " that you have the gift of being able to change yourself into all sorts of creatures you have a mind to; that you can, for example, transform yourself into a lion, or elephant, and the like."

"That is true," answered the Ogre, roughly; "and to convince you, you shall see me now become a lion."

Puss was so terrified at the sight of a lion so near him that he immediately climbed into the gutter, not without much trouble and danger, because of his boots, which were of no use at all to him for walking upon the tiles. A little while after, when Puss saw that the Ogre had resumed his natural form, he came down, and owned he had been very much frightened.

"I have, moreover, been informed," said the Cat, "but I know not how to believe it, that you have also the power to take on you the shape of the smallest animals; for example, to change yourself into a rat or a mouse, but I must own to you I take this to be impossible."

"Impossible!" cried the Ogre; "you shall see." And at the same time he changed himself into a mouse, and began to run about the floor. Puss no sooner perceived this than he fell upon him and ate him up.

Meanwhile, the King, who saw, as he passed, this fine castle of the Ogre's, had a mind to go into it. Puss, who heard the noise of his Majesty's coach coming over the drawbridge, ran out, and said to the King, "Your Majesty is welcome to this castle of my Lord Marquis of Carabas."

"What! my Lord Marquis," cried the King, "and does this castle also belong to you? There can be nothing finer than this courtyard and all the stately buildings which surround it; let us see the interior, if you please."

The Marquis gave his hand to the young Princess, and followed the King, who went first. They passed into the great hall, where they found a magnificent collation, which the Ogre had prepared for his friends, who were that very day to visit him, but dared not to enter, knowing the King was there. His Majesty, charmed with the good qualities of my Lord of Carabas, as was also his daughter, who had fallen violently in love with him, and seeing the vast estate he possessed, said to him : —

"It will be owing to yourself only, my Lord Marquis, if you are not my son-in-law."

The Marquis, with low bows, accepted the honor which his Majesty conferred upon him, and forthwith that very same day married the Princess.

Puss became a great lord, and never ran after mice any more except for his diversion.

RIQUET WITH THE TUFT

ONCE upon a time there was a Queen who had a son so ugly and so misshapen that it was long disputed whether he had human form. A fairy who was at his birth said, however, that he would be very amiable for all that, since he would have uncommon good sense. She even added that it would be in his power, by virtue of a gift she had just then given him, to bestow as much sense as he pleased on the person he loved the best. All this somewhat comforted the poor Queen. It is true that this child no sooner began to talk than he said a thousand pretty things, and in all his actions there was an intelligence that was quite charming. I forgot to tell you that he was born with a little tuft of hair upon his head, which made them call him Riquet[1] with the Tuft, for Riquet was the family name.

Seven or eight years later the Queen of a neighboring kingdom had two daughters who were twins. The first born of these was more beautiful than the day; whereat the Queen was so very glad that those present were afraid that

[1] Rēkā.

her excess of joy would do her harm. The same fairy who was present at the birth of little Riquet with the Tuft was here also, and, to moderate the Queen's gladness, she declared that this little Princess should have no sense at all, but should be as stupid as she was pretty. This mortified the Queen extremely; but afterward she had a far greater sorrow, for the second daughter proved to be very ugly.

"Do not afflict yourself so much, madam," said the fairy. "Your daughter shall have her recompense; she shall have so great a portion of sense that the want of beauty will hardly be perceived."

"God grant it," replied the Queen; "but is there no way to make the eldest, who is so pretty, have any sense?"

"I can do nothing for her, madam, as to sense," answered the fairy, "but everything as to beauty; and as there is nothing I would not do for your satisfaction, I give her for gift that she shall have power to make handsome the person who shall best please her."

As these princesses grew up, their perfections grew with them. All the public talk was of the beauty of the elder and the rare good sense of the younger. It is true also that their defects increased considerably with their age. The younger visibly grew uglier and uglier, and the elder be-

came every day more and more stupid: she either
made no answer at all to what was asked her, or
said something very silly. She was with all this
so unhandy that she could not place four pieces of
china upon the mantelpiece without breaking one
of them, nor drink a glass of water without spill-
ing half of it upon her clothes.

Although beauty is a very great advantage in
young people, the younger sister was always the
more preferred in society. People would indeed
go first to the Beauty to look upon and admire
her, but turn aside soon after to the Wit to hear a
thousand most entertaining and agreeable things;
and it was amazing to see, in less than a quarter
of an hour's time, the elder with not a soul near
her, and the whole company crowding about the
younger. The elder, dull as she was, could not
fail to notice this; and without the slightest re-
gret would have given all her beauty to have half
her sister's wit. The Queen, prudent as she was,
could not help reproaching her several times for
her stupidity, which almost made the poor Princess
die of grief.

One day, as she had hidden herself in a wood
to bewail her misfortune, she saw coming to her
a very disagreeable little man, but most magnificently dressed. This was the young Prince Riquet
with the Tuft, who having fallen in love with her
upon seeing her picture,—many of which were dis-

tributed all the world over, — had left his father's kingdom to have the pleasure of seeing and talking with her. Overjoyed to find her thus alone, he addressed himself to her with all imaginable politeness and respect. Having observed, after he had paid her the ordinary compliments, that she was extremely melancholy, he said to her: —

"I cannot comprehend, madam, how a person so beautiful as you are can be so sorrowful as you seem to be; for though I can boast of having seen a great number of exquisitely charming ladies, I can say that I never beheld any one whose beauty approaches yours."

"You are pleased to say so," answered the Princess, and here she stopped.

"Beauty," replied Riquet with the Tuft, "is such a great advantage, that it ought to take place of all things besides; and since you possess this treasure, I can see nothing that can possibly very much afflict you."

"I had far rather," cried the Princess, "be as ugly as you are, and have sense, than have the beauty I possess, and be as stupid as I am."

"There is nothing, madam," returned he, "shows more that we have good sense than to believe we have none; and it is the nature of that excellent quality that the more people have of it, the more they believe they want it."

"I do not know that," said the Princess; "but

I know very well that I am very senseless, and that vexes me mightily."

"If that be all which troubles you, madam, I can very easily put an end to your affliction."

"And how will you do that?" cried the Princess.

"I have the power, madam," replied Riquet with the Tuft, "to give to that person whom I love best as much good sense as can be had; and as you, madam, are that very person, it will be your fault only if you have not as great a share of it as any one living, provided you will be pleased to marry me."

The Princess was quite confused, and answered not a word.

"I see," replied Riquet with the Tuft, "that this proposal does not please you, and I do not wonder at it; but I will give you a whole year to consider it."

The Princess had so little sense and, at the same time, so great a longing to have some, that she imagined the end of that year would never come, so she accepted the proposal which was made her.

She had no sooner promised Riquet with the Tuft that she would marry him on that day twelvemonth than she found herself quite otherwise than she was before: she had an incredible faculty of speaking whatever she had in her mind in a polite, easy, and natural manner.

She began that moment a very gallant conversation with Riquet with the Tuft, which she kept up at such a rate that Riquet with the Tuft believed he had given her more sense than he had reserved for himself.

When she returned to the palace, the whole court knew not what to think of such a sudden and extraordinary change; for they heard from her now as much sensible discourse and as many infinitely witty phrases as they had heard stupid and silly impertinences before.   The whole court was overjoyed beyond imagination at it.   It pleased all but her younger sister, because, having no longer the advantage of her in respect of wit, she appeared in comparison with her a very disagreeable, homely girl.

The King governed himself by her advice, and would even sometimes hold a council in her apartment.   The news of this change in the Princess spread everywhere; the young princes of the neighboring kingdoms strove all they could to gain her favor, and almost all of them asked her in marriage; but she found not one of them had sense enough for her.   She gave them all a hearing, but would not engage herself to any.

However, there came one so powerful, so rich, so witty, and so handsome that she could not help feeling a strong inclination toward him.   Her father perceived it, and told her that she was her own mistress as to the choice of a husband, and that she might declare her intentions. She thanked her father, and desired him to give her time to consider it.

She went by chance to walk in the same wood where she met Riquet with the Tuft, the more conveniently to think what she ought to do. While she was walking in a profound meditation, she heard a confused noise under her feet, as it were of a great many people busily running backward and forward. Listening more attentively, she heard one say: —

"Bring me that pot," another, "Give me that kettle," and a third, "Put some wood upon the fire."

The ground at the same time opened, and she saw under her feet a great kitchen full of cooks, kitchen helps, and all sorts of officers necessary for a magnificent entertainment. There came out of it a company of cooks, to the number of twenty or thirty, who went to plant themselves about a very long table set up in the forest, with their larding pins in their hands and fox tails in their caps, and began to work, keeping time to a very harmonious tune.

The Princess, all astonished at this sight, asked them for whom they worked.

"For Prince Riquet with the Tuft," said the chief of them, "who is to be married to-morrow."

The Princess, more surprised than ever, and recollecting all at once that it was now that day twelvemonth on which she had promised to marry the Prince Riquet with the Tuft, was ready to sink into the ground.

What made her forget this was that when she made this promise, she was very silly; and having obtained that vast stock of sense which the prince had bestowed upon her, she had entirely forgotten the things she had done in the days of her stupidity. She continued her walk, but had not taken thirty steps before Riquet with the Tuft presented himself to her, gallant and most magnificently dressed, like a prince who was going to be married.

"You see, madam," said he, "I am exact in keeping my word, and doubt not in the least but you are come hither to perform your promise."

"I frankly confess," answered the Princess, "that I have not yet come to a decision in this matter, and I believe I never shall be able to arrive at such a one as you desire."

"You astonish me, madam," said Riquet with the Tuft.

"I can well believe it," said the Princess; "and surely if I had to do with a clown, or a man of no sense, I should find myself very much at a loss. 'A princess always keeps her word,' he would say to me, 'and you must marry me, since you promised to do so.' But as he to whom I talk is the one man in the world who is master of the greatest sense and judgment, I am sure he will hear reason. You know that when I was but a fool I could scarcely make up my mind to marry you; why will you have me, now I have so much judgment as you gave me, come to such a decision which I could not then make up my mind to agree to? If you sincerely thought to make me your wife, you have been greatly in the wrong to deprive me of my dull simplicity, and make me see things much more clearly than I did."

"If a man of no wit and sense," replied Riquet with the Tuft, "would be well received, as you say, in reproaching you for breach of your word, why will you not let me, madam, have the same usage in a matter wherein all the happiness of my life is concerned? Is it reasonable that persons of wit and sense should be in a worse condition than those who have none? Can you pretend this, you who have so great a share, and desired so earnestly to have it? But let us come to the fact, if you please. Putting aside my ugliness and deformity, is there anything in me which displeased you? Are you dissatisfied with my birth, my wit, my humor, or my manners?"

"Not at all," answered the Princess; "I love you and respect you in all that you mention."

"If it be so," said Riquet with the Tuft, "I am

"I AM EXACT IN KEEPING MY WORD."

63

happy, since it is in your power to make me the most amiable of men."

" How can that be?" said the Princess.

" It is done," said Riquet with the Tuft, "if you love me enough to wish it was so; and that you may no ways doubt, madam, of what I say, know that the same fairy who on my birthday gave me for gift the power of making the person who should please me witty and judicious, has in like manner given you for gift the power of making him whom you love and to whom you would grant the favor, to be extremely handsome."

" If it be so," said the Princess, " I wish with all my heart that you may be the most lovable prince in the world, and I bestow my gift on you as much as I am able."

The Princess had no sooner pronounced these words than Riquet with the Tuft appeared to her the finest prince upon earth, the handsomest and most amiable man she ever saw.   Some affirm that it was not the fairy's charms, but love alone, which worked the change.

They say that the Princess, having made due reflection on the perseverance of her lover, his discretion, and all the good qualities of his mind, his wit and judgment, saw no longer the deformity of his body, nor the ugliness of his face; that his hump seemed to her no more than the grand air of one having a broad back, and that whereas till then she saw him limp horribly, she now found it nothing more than a certain sidling air, which charmed her.

They say further that his eyes, which were squinted very much, seemed to her most bright and sparkling, that their irregularity passed in her judgment for a mark of the warmth of his affection, and, in short, that his great red nose was, in her opinion, somewhat martial and heroic in character.

However it was, the Princess promised immediately to marry him, on condition that he obtained the King's consent. The King, knowing that his daughter highly esteemed Riquet with the Tuft, whom he knew also for a most sage and judicious prince, received him for his son-in-law with pleasure, and the next morning their nuptials were celebrated, as Riquet with the Tuft had foreseen, and according to the orders he had given a long time before.

BLUE BEARD

Once upon a time there was a man who had fine houses, both in town and country, a deal of silver and gold plate, carved furniture, and coaches gilded all over. But unhappily this man had a blue beard, which made him so ugly and so terrible that all the women and girls ran away from him.

One of his neighbors, a lady of quality, had two daughters who were perfect beauties. He asked for one of them in marriage, leaving to her the choice of which she would bestow on him. They would neither of them have him, and they sent him backward and forward from one to the other, neither being able to make up her mind to marry a man who had a blue beard. Another thing which made them averse to him was that he had already married several wives, and nobody knew what had become of them.

Blue Beard, to become better acquainted, took them, with their mother and three or four of their best friends, with some young people of the neighborhood to one of his country seats, where they stayed a whole week.

There was nothing going on but pleasure parties, hunting, fishing, dancing, mirth, and feasting. Nobody went to bed, but all passed the night in playing pranks on each other. In short, everything succeeded so well that the youngest daughter began to think that the beard of the master of the house was not so very blue, and that he was a very civil gentleman. So as soon as they returned home, the marriage was concluded.

About a month afterward Blue Beard told his wife that he was obliged to take a country journey for six weeks at least, upon business of great importance. He desired her to amuse herself well in his absence, to send for her friends, to take them into the country, if she pleased, and to live well wherever she was.

" Here," said he, " are the keys of the two great warehouses wherein I have my best furniture: these are of the room where I keep my silver and gold plate, which is not in everyday use; these open my safes, which hold my money, both gold and silver; these my caskets of jewels; and this is the master-key to all my apartments. But as for this little key, it is the key of the closet at the end of the great gallery on the ground floor. Open them all; go everywhere; but as for that little closet, I forbid you to enter it, and I promise you surely that, if you open it, there's nothing that you may not expect from my anger."

She promised to obey exactly all his orders; and he, after having embraced her, got into his coach and proceeded on his journey.

Her neighbors and good friends did not stay to be sent for by the new-married lady, so great was their impatience to see all the riches of her house, not daring to come while her husband was there, because of his blue beard, which frightened them. They at once ran through all the rooms, closets, and wardrobes, which were so fine and rich, and each seemed to surpass all others. They went up into the warehouses, where was the best and richest furniture; and they could not sufficiently admire the number and beauty of the tapestry, beds, couches, cabinets, stands, tables, and looking-glasses, in which you might see your-self from head to foot. Some of them were framed with glass, others with silver, plain and gilded, the most beautiful and the most magnifi-cent ever seen.

They ceased not to praise and envy the happi-ness of their friend, who, in the meantime, was not at all amused by looking upon all these rich things, because of her impatience to go and open the closet on the ground floor. Her curiosity was so great that, without considering how uncivil it was to leave her guests, she went down a little back staircase, with such excessive haste that twice or thrice she came near breaking her neck.

"IF YOU OPEN IT, THERE'S NOTHING YOU MAY NOT EXPECT FROM MY ANGER."

Having reached the closet-door, she stood still for some time, thinking of her husband's orders, and considering that unhappiness might attend her if she was disobedient; but the temptation was so strong she could not overcome it. She then took the little key, and opened the door, trembling. At first she could not see anything plainly, because the windows were shut. After some moments she began to perceive that several dead women were scattered about the floor. (These were all the wives whom Blue Beard had married and murdered, one after the other, because they did not obey his orders about the closet on the ground floor.) She thought she surely would die for fear, and the key, which she pulled out of the lock, fell out of her hand.

After having somewhat recovered from the shock, she picked up the key, locked the door, and went upstairs into her chamber to compose herself; but she could not rest, so much was she frightened.

Having observed that the key of the closet was stained, she tried two or three times to wipe off the stain, but the stain would not come out. In vain did she wash it, and even rub it with soap and sand. The stain still remained, for the key was a magic key, and she could never make it quite clean; when the stain was gone off from one side, it came again on the other.

Blue Beard returned from his journey that same evening, and said he had received letters upon the road, informing him that the business which called him away was ended to his advantage. His wife did all she could to convince him she was delighted at his speedy return.

Next morning he asked her for the keys, which she gave him, but with such a trembling hand that he easily guessed what had happened.

" How is it," said he, "that the key of my closet is not among the rest?"

" I must certainly," said she, " have left it upstairs upon the table."

" Do not fail," said Blue Beard, "to bring it to me presently."

After having put off doing it several times, she was forced to bring him the key. Blue Beard, having examined it, said to his wife: —

" How comes this stain upon the key?"

" I do not know," cried the poor woman, paler than death.

" You do not know!" replied Blue Beard. " I very well know. You wished to go into the cabinet? Very well, madam; you shall go in, and take your place among the ladies you saw there."

She threw herself weeping at her husband's feet, and begged his pardon with all the signs of a true repentance for her disobedience. She would have melted a rock, so beautiful and sorrowful was she; but Blue Beard had a heart harder than any stone.

"You must die, madam," said he, "and that at once."

"Since I must die," answered she, looking upon him with her eyes all bathed in tears, "give me some little time to say my prayers."

"I give you," replied Blue Beard, "half a quarter of an hour, but not one moment more."

When she was alone she called out to her sister, and said to her: —

"Sister Anne," — for that was her name, — "go up, I beg you, to the top of the tower, and look if my brothers are not coming; they promised me they would come to-day, and if you see them, give them a sign to make haste."

Her sister Anne went up to the top of the tower, and the poor afflicted wife cried out from time to time: —

"Anne, sister Anne, do you see any one coming?"

And sister Anne said: —

"I see nothing but the sun, which makes a dust, and the grass, which looks green."

In the meanwhile Blue Beard, holding a great sabre in his hand, cried to his wife as loud as he could: —

"Come down instantly, or I shall come up to you."

"One moment longer, if you please," said his wife; and then she cried out very softly, "Anne, sister Anne, dost thou see anybody coming?"

And sister Anne answered: —

"I see nothing but the sun, which makes a dust, and the grass, which is green."

"Come down quickly," cried Blue Beard, "or I will come up to you."

"I am coming," answered his wife; and then she cried, "Anne, sister Anne, dost thou not see any one coming?"

"I see," replied sister Anne, "a great dust, which comes from this side."

"Are they my brothers?"

"Alas! no, my sister, I see a flock of sheep."

"Will you not come down?" cried Blue Beard.

"One moment longer," said his wife, and then she cried out, "Anne, sister Anne, dost thou see nobody coming?"

"I see," said she, "two horsemen, but they are yet a great way off."

"God be praised," replied the poor wife, joyfully; "they are my brothers; I will make them a sign, as well as I can, for them to make haste."

Then Blue Beard bawled out so loud that he made the whole house tremble. The distressed wife came down, and threw herself at his feet, all in tears, with her hair about her shoulders.

"All this is of no help to you," says Blue Beard;

"you must die"; then, taking hold of her hair with one hand, and lifting up his sword in the air with the other, he was about to take off her head. The poor lady, turning about to him, and looking at him with dying eyes, desired him to afford her one little moment to her thoughts.

" No, no," said he, " commend thyself to God," and again lifting his arm —

At this moment there was such a loud knocking at the gate that Blue Beard stopped suddenly. The gate was opened, and presently entered two horsemen, who, with sword in hand, ran directly to Blue Beard. He knew them to be his wife's brothers, one a dragoon, the other a musketeer. He ran away immediately, but the two brothers pursued him so closely that they overtook him before he could get to the steps of the porch. There they ran their swords through his body, and left him dead. The poor wife was almost as dead as her husband, and had not strength enough to arise and welcome her brothers.

Blue Beard had no heirs, and so his wife became mistress of all his estate. She made use of one portion of it to marry her sister Anne to a young gentleman who had loved her a long while; another portion to buy captains' commissions for her brothers; and the rest to marry herself to a very worthy gentleman, who made her forget the sorry time she had passed with Blue Beard.

THE FAIRY

ONCE upon a time there was a widow who had two daughters. The elder was so much like her, both in looks and character, that whoever saw the daughter saw the mother. They were both so disagreeable and so proud that there was no living with them. The younger, who was the very picture of her father for sweetness of temper and virtue, was withal one of the most beautiful girls ever seen. As people naturally love their own likeness, this mother doted on her elder daughter, and at the same time had a great aversion for the younger. She made her eat in the kitchen and work continually.

Among other things, this unfortunate child had to go twice a day to draw water more than a mile and a half from the house, and bring home a pitcherful of it. One day, as she was at this fountain, there came to her a poor woman, who begged of her to let her drink.

"Oh, yes, with all my heart, Goody," said this pretty little girl. Rinsing the pitcher at once, she took some of the clearest water from the fountain, and gave it to her, holding up the pitcher all the while, that she might drink the easier.

The good woman having drunk, said to her : —

" You are so pretty, so good and courteous, that I cannot help giving you a gift." For this was a fairy, who had taken the form of a poor country-woman, to see how far the civility and good manners of this pretty girl would go. " I will give you for gift," continued the Fairy, " that, at every word you speak, there shall come out of your mouth either a flower or a jewel."

When this pretty girl returned, her mother scolded at her for staying so long at the fountain.

" I beg your pardon, mamma," said the poor girl, " for not making more haste."

And in speaking these words there came out of her mouth two roses, two pearls, and two large diamonds.

" What is it I see there ? " said her mother, quite astonished. " I think pearls and diamonds come out of the girl's mouth ! How happens this, my child ? "

This was the first time she had ever called her " my child."

The girl told her frankly all the matter, not without dropping out great numbers of diamonds.

" Truly," cried the mother, " I must send my own dear child thither. Fanny, look at what comes out of your sister's mouth when she speaks. Would you not be glad, my dear, to have the same gift ? You have only to go and draw water

"WITH ALL MY HEART, GOODY."

77,

out of the fountain, and when a poor woman **asks**
you to let her drink, to give it to her **very**
civilly."

" I should like to see myself going to the fountain to draw water," said this ill-bred minx.

" I insist you shall go," said the mother, "and
that instantly."

She went, but grumbled all the way, taking
with her the best silver tankard in the house.

She no sooner reached the fountain than she
saw coming out of the wood, a magnificently
dressed lady, who came up to her, and asked to
drink. This was the same fairy who had appeared
to her sister, but she had now taken the air and
dress of a princess, to see how far this girl's rude-
ness would go.

" Am I come hither," said the proud, ill-bred
girl, " to serve you with water, pray? I suppose
this silver tankard was brought purely for your
ladyship, was it? However, you may drink out
of it, if you have a fancy."

" You are scarcely polite," answered the fairy,
without anger. " Well, then, since you are so dis-
obliging, I give you for gift that at every word
you speak there shall come out of your mouth a
snake or a toad."

So soon as her mother saw her coming, **she**
cried out : —

" Well, daughter? "

" Well, mother ? " answered the unhappy girl, throwing out of her mouth a viper and a toad.

"Oh, mercy!" cried the mother, "what is it I see? It is her sister who has caused all this, but she shall pay for it," and immediately she ran to beat her. The poor child fled away from her, and went to hide herself in the forest near by.

The King's son, who was returning from the chase, met her, and seeing her so beautiful, asked her what she did there alone and why she cried.

"Alas! sir, my mother has turned me out of doors."

The King's son, who saw five or six pearls and as many diamonds come out of her mouth, desired her to tell him how that happened. She told him the whole story. The King's son fell in love with her, and, considering that such a gift was worth more than any marriage portion another bride could bring, conducted her to the palace of the King, his father, and there married her.

As for her sister, she made herself so much hated that her own mother turned her out of doors. The miserable girl, after wandering about and finding no one to take her in, went to a corner of the wood, and there died.

LITTLE RED RIDING-HOOD

ONCE upon a time there lived in a certain village a little country girl, the prettiest creature that ever was seen. Her mother was very fond of her, and her grandmother loved her still more. This good woman made for her a little red riding-hood, which became the girl so well that everybody called her Little Red Riding-hood.

One day her mother, having made some custards, said to her: —

" Go, my dear, and see how your grandmother does, for I hear she has been very ill; carry her a custard and this little pot of butter."

Little Red Riding-hood set out immediately to go to her grandmother's, who lived in another village.

As she was going through the wood, she met Gaffer Wolf, who had a very great mind to eat her up; but he dared not, because of some fagot-makers hard by in the forest. He asked her whither she was going. The poor child, who did not know that it was dangerous to stay and hear a wolf talk, said to him: —

" I am going to see my grandmother, and carry

her a custard and a little pot of butter from my
mamma."

"Does she live far off?" said the Wolf.

"Oh, yes," answered Little Red Riding-hood;
"it is beyond that mill you see there, the first
house you come to in the village."

"Well," said the Wolf, "and I'll go and see her,
too. I'll go this way, and you go that, and we
shall see who will be there first."

The Wolf began to run as fast as he could,
taking the shortest way, and the little girl went
by the longest way, amusing herself by gathering
nuts, running after butterflies, and making nose-
gays of such little flowers as she met with. The
Wolf was not long before he reached the old
woman's house. He knocked at the door — tap,
tap, tap.

"Who's there?" called the grandmother.

"Your grandchild, Little Red Riding-hood,"
replied the Wolf, imitating her voice, "who has
brought a custard and a little pot of butter sent
to you by mamma."

The good grandmother, who was in bed, because she was somewhat ill, cried out: —

"Pull the bobbin, and the latch will go up."

The Wolf pulled the bobbin, and the door
opened. He fell upon the good woman and ate
her up in no time, for he had not eaten anything
for more than three days. He then shut the

door, went into the grandmother's bed, and waited for Little Red Riding-hood, who came sometime afterward and knocked at the door — tap, tap, tap.

"Who's there?" called the Wolf.

Little Red Riding-hood, hearing the big voice of the Wolf, was at first afraid; but thinking her grandmother had a cold, answered: —

"'Tis your grandchild, Little Red Riding-hood, who has brought you a custard and a little pot of butter sent to you by mamma."

The Wolf cried out to her, softening his voice a little: —

"Pull the bobbin, and the latch will go up."

Little Red Riding-hood pulled the bobbin, and the door opened.

The Wolf, seeing her come in, said to her, hiding himself under the bedclothes: —

"Put the custard and the little pot of butter upon the stool, and come and lie down with me."

Little Red Riding-hood undressed herself and went into bed, where she was much surprised to see how her grandmother looked in her night-clothes.

She said to her: —

"Grandmamma, what great arms you have got!"

"That is the better to hug thee, my dear."

"Grandmamma, what great legs you have got!"

"HE FELL UPON THE GOOD WOMAN."

" That is to run the better, my child."

" Grandmamma, what great ears you have got ! "

" That is to hear the better, my child."

" Grandmamma, what great eyes you have got ! "

" It is to see the better, my child."

" Grandmamma, what great teeth you have got ! "

" That is to eat thee up."

And, saying these words, this wicked Wolf fell upon Little Red Riding-hood, and ate her all up.

NOTE

THE eight stories contained in this volume are first found in print in French in a magazine entitled, *Receuil de pièces curieuses et nouvelles tant en prose qu'en vers*, which was published by Adrian Moetjens at The Hague in 1696–1697. They were immediately afterward published at Paris in a volume entitled, *Histoires ou Contes du Temps Passé, avec des Moralites — Contes de ma mère l'Oie.*

The earliest translation into English has been found in a little book containing both the English and French, entitled, "Tales of Passed Times, by Mother Goose. With Morals. Written in French by M. (Charles) Perrault, and Englished by R. S. Gent."

Who R. S. was and when he made his translation we can only conjecture. Mr. Andrew Lang, in his "Perrault's Popular Tales" (p. xxxiv), writes: "An English version translated by Mr. Samber, printed for J. Pote, was advertised, Mr. Austin Dobson tells me, in the *Monthly Chronicle*, March, 1729."

These stories which may be said to be as old as the race itself — certainly their germs are to be found in the oldest literature and among the oldest folk-tales in the world — were orally current in France and the neighboring countries in nearly the form in which Perrault wrote them for very many years; and an interesting account of the various forms in which they are found in the

85

literature and folklore of other nations before Perrault's time is given in *Les Contes de ma mère l'Oie avant Perrault*, by Charles Deulin, Paris, E. Dentu, 1878.

In this book Mr. Deulin inclines to the view that the stories as first published by Perrault were not really written by him, but by his little son of ten or eleven, to whom Perrault told the stories as he had gathered them up with the intention of rendering them in verse after the manner of La Fontaine. The lad had an excellent memory, much natural wit, and a great gift of expression. He loved the stories his father told him and thoroughly enjoyed the task his father set him of rewriting them from memory, as an exercise. This was so happily done, in such a fresh, artless, and engaging style, exactly befitting the subjects of the stories, that the father found the son's version better than the one he had contemplated and gave that to the world instead.

These stories made their way slowly in England at first, but in the end they nearly eclipsed the native fairy tales and legends, which, owing to Puritan influence, had been frowned upon and discouraged until they were remembered only in the remoter districts, and told only by the few who had not come under its sway. Indeed, the Puritanical objection to nursery lore of all kinds still lingers in some corners of England.

The stories of Perrault came in just when the severer manifestations of Puritanism were beginning to decline, and they have since become as much a part of English fairy lore as the old English folk and fairy tales themselves. These latter, thanks to Mr. Joseph Jacob, Mr. Andrew Lang, Mr. E. S. Hartland, and others, have been unearthed and revived, and prove to have lost nothing of their power of taking hold upon the minds of the little folk.

Perrault says of his collection that it is certain these stories excite in the children who read them the desire to resemble those characters who become happy, and at the same time they inspire them with the fear of the consequences which happen to those who do ill deeds; and he claims that they all contain a very distinct moral which is more or less evident to all who read them.

Emerson says: "What Nature at one time provides for use, she afterwards turns to ornament," and Herbert Spencer, following out this idea, remarks that "the fairy lore, which in times past was matter of grave belief and held sway over people's conduct, has since been transformed into ornament for *The Midsummer Night's Dream*, *The Tempest*, *The Fairy Queen*, and endless small tales and poems; and still affords subjects for children's story books, amuses boys and girls, and becomes matter for jocose allusion."

Thus, also, Sir Walter Scott, in a note to "The Lady of the Lake," says: "The mythology of one period would appear to pass into the romance of the next, and that into the nursery tales of subsequent ages," and Max Muller, in his "Chips from a German Workshop," says: "The gods of ancient mythology were changed into the demigods and heroes of ancient epic poetry, and these demigods again became at a later age the principal characters of our nursery tales."

These thoughts may help to a better understanding of some of the uses of such stories and of their proper place in children's reading.   C. W.

Ingram Content Group UK Ltd.
Milton Keynes UK
UKHW020119200523
422059UK00005B/64

9 781015 722378